I Conversion

The way of prayer of St. Ignatius, the founder of the Society of Jesus, has been very influential since the sixteenth century. It marked the change from a generally interior, monastic form of spirituality, symbolised by withdrawal from the world (often literally), to what we recognise as a modern idea of the Church *in* the world (the well-used phrase 'in the world but not of it'), i.e. to a concept of Christianity which *includes* the world. This necessarily involves a world-view consistent with Christianity, a way of looking at the world in accordance with Christian principles — and that is often where the difficulties come in.

How do we know the 'Christian' way of looking at, say, political problems, or issues like rail disputes? Is there a 'Christian' view or is there right (and wrong) on both sides? But here Ignatius goes on to consider *discernment* — and this is a key word for him. The only way to live in the world is to grow in discerning between good and evil influences, or between good and less good influences; to see more and more clearly what the real issues are in order to throw our weight more and more often behind *right* choices. This is by no means easy — nor is it something which grows overnight. Hence the need to grow closer and closer to Our Lord — to be converted at more and deeper levels of our selves and personalities — to root out self-interested motives — in order to see more clearly and choose more freely the Right — and so to serve God and give Him more glory. And that is what Ignatius' prayer is all about.

In this booklet we shall be looking at his methods and seeing from his own life-story how he arrived at them. The point about prayer is that it should be prayed, not just read about; so there will also be practical suggestions of topics to be prayed about and ways and methods of doing so.

St. Ignatius was born some time in 1491 into one of the 24 noble Basque families, at the family castle of Loyola. He was christened Inigo Lopez de Loyola; he took the name 'Ignatius' years later in Paris. The extreme power and social significance of these families was in decline over against the growing democracy of the cities and the powerful monarchy of Castille. Nevertheless — they seem to us rather a bloodthirsty collection! Both grandfather and father had sworn the oath of loyalty to Ferdinand and Isabella — loyalty to the Crown was a mark of the family. We will see how these traits were translated into *his* Christian thought as he transferred his loyalty and devotion to Christ the King and Captain of all.

Remember also that while Inigo was a baby Columbus set sail: Inigo was born at the beginning of the New World.

1

His mother had seven sons and four daughters. He was the last and as his mother died before he was seven, was brought up by his sister-in-law, whom he adored. He was, of course, brought up in the Church before the Reformation. He grew up rather wild. He was a true Basque — hard-headed and passionate; he enjoyed dancing. A poet said of the Basques, 'They dwell on the iron mountains, strong in action and silent of work, and with their iron Spain has won her gold'. Oak and iron are Basque symbols. Yet again this is important in our understanding of his later spirituality. We say that 'grace builds on nature' i.e. that Our Lord takes our human gifts and abilities and uses them in His own purposes. Our new Christian self and identity will reflect our 'natural' selves. He does not destroy our human personalities. We will see how this was true in Ignatius' case.

When he was 15 or 16 he was taken into the household of the master of the royal treasury. He spent ten years there as a page and elegant young courtier before his master was disgraced and he transferred to another's service. He enjoyed the life — got up to all sorts of mischief — dreamed of doing great deeds, acquiring honour and glory — dallied in courtly romances. His only desire was a military career. He says of himself that he 'was reckless at games, in adventures with women, in brawls and deeds of arms. He was assailed and overcome by temptations of the flesh'. Under his new master he went to war and finally became involved in war against the French, defending the town of Pamplona in northern Spain. The garrison wanted to surrender but, characteristically, Ignatius encouraged resistance until finally he was hit by a cannon ball which shattered his leg on the wall of the town and they had to give in. This was on Whit Monday 1521. He was cared for by the French for two weeks and then carried back to his castle where he was looked after by his sister-in-law. The bone grew crooked: because he was afraid it would look ugly in silk trousers he insisted it was broken and re-set. He was very near death and received the Last Sacraments but then gradually recovered. Convalescence was long and slow and he had nothing to read. So he asked for books and was brought a Life of Christ and a book of the Lives of the Saints. A new world opened before him.

As he read, Inigo was struck by the passionate love that the saints had for Christ. The desire formed in him to imitate the saints: to do penance for his past life and to serve Christ. He was poised between the old life and the new. When he thought and dreamt of his old life and ambitions, he felt pleasure, but he noticed that it left him tired and depressed. When he thought of serving Our Lord, he experienced comfort and peace and happiness that stayed with him after he stopped thinking. This experience — of comfort or of depression — formed the basis of his later thinking on discernment and how to distinguish between two courses of action, both of which seemed good. He never says that it is wrong to enjoy created things — only that their benefit is only relative: they will never bring deep or lasting happiness and fulfilment. So — he was converted. He had a vision of the

PRAYER FOR OUR TIME

The Way of St Ignatius Loyola

Marion Morgan

Mirfield Publications

ISBN 0−902834−19−3
First printed privately 1982
This edition 1987
Printed and bound by Carmelite Monastery
Quidenham Norfolk England

Madonna and Child which confirmed his thinking. He eventually recovered and set off (rather dramatically) on a donkey with no clearer idea than to beg his way across Spain and go as a pilgrim to Jerusalem.

At this stage his conversion meant little more than that he had exchanged 'worldly' ambitions for 'holy' ambitions. Later on he would recognise this and see that *we* often tell *Christ* that we are going to serve Him, asking His help as an addition. He realised later that conversion is an ongoing process: a process of deepening, over and over again, our commitment to and union with Christ, so that in the end His will — truly *His* will — is done in us with our glad consent, but with self-interest and our own motives rooted out. I think that is why conversion is often rather off-putting: the new convert is still largely 'unpurified' and his zeal is mixed in very much with his own emotions and desires and the results can be rather strange. Ignatius' enthusiasm and even excesses were later moderated and tempered without in any way reducing his deep and lasting commitment; rather, making it a much more worthwhile thing. A conversion experience such as his is only the beginning of a long process. For others the process can be going on all the time and an actual conscious conversion can go almost unnoticed: it can be the sum of many small choices for Good.

Ignatius arrived at Montserrat, the other side of Spain: a Benedictine monastery and shrine to Mary, set on the top of some odd-shaped mountains. He examined his conscience for three days, made a full confession, did a night's vigil and offered himself totally to the service of Almighty God. He gave his fine clothes away, bought pilgrim's attire of rope, hemp-linen and sandals and set off for the neighbouring small town of Manresa. Here he took up residence in a Dominican convent and spent much of his time teaching the children in the streets and caring for the sick in the hospital: tasks which were not at all similar to such tasks today and which must have meant severe penance for someone brought up fastidiously like Ignatius. But he found a cave by the side of the river, looking across at the high serrated edge of Montserrat, and here he spent hours in prayer and meditation, becoming more and more unkempt. In the end he was almost in despair and cried to God for help. He had completely come to the end of his own efforts and resources. And God answered him. Ignatius was given visions of the Trinity, of the love of God in Creation; of the love of Our Lord and His redemptive mission. It was here, that the core of his thinking and enlightenment that eventually gave rise to the book of the Spiritual Exercises took place.

Leaving the story of Ignatius here temporarily and turning to prayer, the first topic for our attention is the idea of the love of God shown through Creation.

Ignatius suggests as a method for prayer:—

1. putting ourselves in the presence of God;

3

2. making an introductory prayer for the grace we are looking for, e.g. deepening our love or commitment, a growth in understanding;
3. then the meditation itself (decide on a set time beforehand, e.g. 20 mins; 30 mins, or an hour perhaps, but try not to cut it short once you have decided);
4. then what is called the 'colloquy' or little chat with Our Lord;
5. finally, thanksgiving and perhaps a set prayer, e.g. the Our Father.

It is always good to start with a Scripture reading. Ones you might use for such a meditation on Creation are Is. 43.1−7; or Creation psalms (e.g. Ps. 8 or 104) or even some of the last chapters of Job. But I personally find helpful the first 3 chapters of Genesis. Don't get bogged down on the details: go for the truths — that Creation is *good*; that something has gone wrong and was intended to be good. And man is part of this creation which was created in joy: 'The morning stars sang together and all the sons of God shouted with joy'.(Job 38.7).

Man was created with a purpose, and fulfilling that purpose brings meaning into our lives. Meaning derives from God, and is given to us as an experience when we choose finites in accordance with His will. We break through the finite and taste the infinite; put deep roots down into the eternal. Meaninglessness comes from engaging in things cut off from His will and purpose. And what is His will and purpose? He gave man dominion over the earth. We are to be stewards of the good things of creation. We are to till the ground; harness the natural forces; create and so dis-cover (make manifest) that-of-God in Creation which lies hidden until we develop it, inspired and helped by Him; like machines; and speed; and steam; electricity; technology. Without man's efforts these aspects and truths about God would have been left undisclosed. There *is* a beauty to be found in technology, e.g. aircraft in flight. Another example, that of a cut diamond as against a rough diamond, also illustrates that God is revealed through man's efforts with nature. But it is all relative and can be thrown down and destroyed. History and tradition; law; order; authority; cultures; service; all *point* to Him but *are* not Him. They are His image; His creation. Thus our knowledge of Him and of His ways is slowly extended.

Man was created with a purpose and we ignore our purpose at our own peril. All things were created for a purpose, which we can try and discover but which we cannot create and which we have no right to twist and pervert. When we twist and pervert things against their true purposes we contribute to the sinfulness and falsity of the world.

We must remember always that we are stewards of Creation, not owners. It is one day to be given back, in Christ, to the Father. It is subject to recall. We were given dominion, but not the stuff of Creation itself. 'The earth is the Lord's and the fullness thereof' (Ps. 24.1).Tithing in the Old Testament acknowledges God's ownership.

And what of man? Yes — as part of Creation he also is owned by God. It may be that in giving us free-will He gave us to ourselves; but man, if he is wise, will guess the riddle and give himself back to God and hence find joy, meaning and true freedom.

Otherwise — and anyway — he is always subject to God's final jurisdiction and is accountable to Him, because God *is* God, and He makes the rules. Man was given the earth to till but will have to render account of his stewardship.

This leads on to the fundamental principle underlying all Ignatius' thought and writing. It is this: —

'Man is created to praise, reverence and serve God Our Lord and by this means to save his soul.

The other things on the face of the earth are created for man to help him in attaining the end for which he is created.

Hence man is to make use of them in as far as they help him to attain his end, and he must rid himself of them in as far as they prove a hindrance to him. Therefore we must make ourselves indifferent to all created things, as far as we are allowed free choice and are not under any prohibition. Consequently, as far as we are concerned, we should not prefer health to sickness, riches to poverty, honour to dishonour, a long life to a short life. The same holds for all other things.

Our one desire and choice should be what is more conducive to the end for which we are created'.

The latter part of this will be looked at later; but we might observe here that this sort of meditation can lead to an awareness of God's greatness and our presumption — *my* presumption! We are made to praise Him; to till the earth; to create; to utter His greatness. So often we think that *we* have done everything!

Reverence — means to acknowledge in our heart the truth of matters. That *He* is great and I am His creature.

To save his soul — means to achieve the purpose for which we were created which is to share His glory and bliss in heaven.

Man is created — man *was made so* in the beginning. It is part and parcel of what man *is*.

'Serving the Lord' does not necessarily mean going to church and serving on committees. That may be part of it and may come later. It has more to do, first, with acknowledging our relationship to Him. The first act of worship is recorded in Gen. 1.28. The man and woman, newly made, stood before God. And He blessed them. Only then did He give them dominion. He gave: He took the initiative; and He blessed them. It is a simple picture; it applies to everyone, and we can find rest in it. Action comes later. First, we were created by God — we are His — and He blesses us.

God Our Father, we pray for your help, the help of your Son and of the

Holy Spirit, that our view of the basic goodness of creation may be restored to us and deepened; that we may learn to see and value ourselves as your creation and as temples of your Spirit; that you will restore to us our sense of true purpose; and give us the grace to give ourselves back to you. We ask this through Jesus Christ Our Lord.

II Reconciliation

We now consider the problem of sin, the problem that Ignatius wrestled and grappled with in the cave at Manresa. The whole of the spirituality of St. Ignatius and the Jesuits should be understood in the context that Creation is basically good and to be enjoyed in all its aspects for God's greater glory. All man's activities in its regard: his buildings, his inventions, his social ordering, his sport, have the potential for being fully good. All such activity gives praise and glory to God, i.e. it tells us more about God who created the raw materials, and man, and man's brain; so that man, in discovering himself and the world, might discover more of the God who made it, might discover it, bring it to light, make it visible. But St. Ignatius saw what we all see — that so much of man's activity is enmeshed in self-interest and exploitation of others: that greed and complacency and dishonesty and corruption and immorality are rife. Sin creeps in and spoils all things: enterprises; beauty; relationships. Sooner or later, everything we begin or are involved in begins to spoil or go wrong on us and we have to begin really working to keep its original freshness and goodness intact. Even Creation itself seems out of gear with itself at times. We have only to read the news, or look at the international or national, or local scene to see pain and disruption caused always, in broad terms, by sin.

The secular world has very largely thrown out faith. We try and understand the world on its own merits and in its own context. And although we can learn a certain amount by doing that, until we acknowledge that we are accountable to God who first created us and then redeemed us, we will never really see it clearly.

Ignatius also saw in himself that much of his own enthusiasm and desire for heavenly glory was rooted in just the same pride and ambition as his earlier earthly dreams. Pride and ambition of the wrong sort always mean the end of personal happiness and real personhood. He realised that *he* was deciding the way *he* was going to serve the Lord, with little reference to what the *Lord* may have wanted. This is a very common danger for us as well. It is so easy to say 'yes' to some good work or other without very much careful thought and then find we are unable to see or pay attention to Our Lord when He is in fact beckoning us into some other direction. So, much of the Spiritual Exercises, indeed roughly one week out of the four, is designed to help a person see and discern where sin or self-interest or even just lack of thought or carelessness are spoiling his life and his happiness, his relationships and his service. It helps us to see where these things are tiring us and making us unable to enjoy God's good Creation and to work happily and joyfully within it. He wants to restore to life the joy which sin destroys, and to make us more receptive to the Life 'abundant and free' brought to us by Christ.

Ignatius recognises that each time we sin it results in a blindness that prevents us from seeing that particular act as a fault in ourselves. If I do something wrong, I can find a hundred reasons for saying that for me, at that time, it was not a sin! I can justify it! It does not seem wrong to me. That is why other people's faults and failings are always so obvious to us but our own are so hard to identify. Sin is always unattractive, so we notice and talk about it in others but cannot bear to see it in ourselves. But it does affect all of us, so let us be kind about it and also courageous enough to look at our own lives. To overcome the difficulty, Ignatius recommends starting with a prayer to the Holy Spirit asking Him to show us our hidden and secret sins.

There are various ways of making an examination of conscience. We can start with the obvious sins, anything which springs to mind immediately, making us feel uncomfortable. Or we can ask a few questions, e.g. Do I depress other people? Are there aspects of my life that depress other people? What things that I do depress me? Why? It is helpful to think of different aspects of our life: home; work; social relationships; church activities; habits of prayer. If I am thinking of the whole of my life, I might divide it into sections: pre-school (just in case anything still worries me!); school; family; adolescence; marriage; work; etc. It may be helpful to jot points down on paper. We can also consider general attitudes: Do I recognise other points of view? Do I condemn out of hand large sections of the population through prejudice? Am I complacent? Do I avoid issues through cowardice or laziness rather than from discretion? These are all simply suggestions and in no way meant to be comprehensive!

Perhaps we should also remember Our Lord's firm statement that unless we forgive others we shall not ourselves be forgiven (Matt. 6.14, 15; 18.35). Do I bear grudges? Is there anyone I don't speak to? Do I remember and acknowledge my total dependence on God? Do I acknowledge His ownership of me — a two-fold ownership, if I will admit it. He made me; He redeemed me. He is all. I am nothing. There is no room for two powers. He gives me to myself; enables me to live and work and have my being. What does that say about my pride and presumption? How hard it is to say 'I am proud'.

The 'examen', the self-examination, can be included in a meditation. Christ Our Lord is most merciful! There are some lovely stories and parables that we can think about. We could use the method suggested in part I, choosing a particular story to think about. When thinking about a story, Ignatius tells us really to imagine it and put ourselves into it. He tells us to see the scene; to smell the smells which will be there, e.g. animals, or people, or fish, or grass etc.; and to hear the conversations which are taking place. We are to choose a character that we will be in the scene. So, if we think about the Prodigal Son, we could be the father, or the older son, or, of course, the younger son himself. This way, a meditation can really 'take off' for us, and can be very revealing and helpful. The Prodigal Son (Lk 15.11 − 32) is a good story to think about in this context of 'examen' and reconciliation. He sets off and goes to the city − how would *I* debauch myself in this city? What would I do? And when I finish up in a pigsty . . . what would my pigsty look like? One Jesuit I know advises you really to get inside your pigsty! Look all round! What is it *like*? Look into the dark corners of it and don't be afraid.

Another story as an alternative would be that of a leper coming to Christ. Feel how dirty and scabrous and rotten you are . . . and yet you are crying out for healing. 'If You want to You can make me whole.' 'Of course I want to . . .' (Matt. 8.3).

Or a way I find helpful is to come to Him just as I am, but thinking of Him as a boy of 12, perhaps sitting on a hillside with me. I would then have to face up to the candour and perception and the question of such a young adult. What do I know that He does not know and that I would be ashamed for Him to know? Even thinking of Him as a baby in the nativity scene can make us uncomfortably aware of our own crustiness and cynicism.

Do not be discouraged! The more He shows you, the more He loves you, and the more chance you have of being sorry and being healed.

Perhaps our problem − and I believe it is a common one − is that we do not feel sinful. We lead good lives and try our best − what more can we do? Thank God and praise Him for His grace in helping us! Be encouraged − He is with us in our efforts. But when we do find things or attitudes we are sorry about and which we recognise as unworthy of our high calling as human beings and as Christians − as His Creation − then we can make what Roman Catholics call a 'prayer of contrition', a 'sorry' prayer. This is the one we teach the children: 'O my God, I am very sorry for having offended you and with the help of your grace I will not sin again'. Then, in the tradition of our own Church denomination, we can make our confession of sin and receive absolution, either together or individually. And we are free again.

Another point I should like to make is that Roman Catholics make a distinction between what is called guilt and culpability, i.e. something may be objectively wrong (for example, stealing a loaf of bread) but the person concerned may bear minimal guilt and responsibility for the act (e.g. he may have a starving family). It would be a great pity if I were so concerned about my personal guilt (or, more usually, a friend's or relative's) in a particular matter, that I allowed my judgement to be clouded as to whether or not such and such a matter was *objectively* wrong, i.e. not the best way for a human being to act in order to be true to his potentially noble and great nature. The problem is particularly acute in matters of sexual morality. Because I do not want to condemn that particular person for the irregularity involved (because

8

I understand how he was forced, persuaded into it, etc.) I say that it is not wrong anyway. This is how our whole thinking can get very muddled and we cease to hold effectively the high standards which do in fact lead to health and happiness both for the individual and for society.

St. Ignatius was very practical regarding the examen, and also strict. Much later, he would ask his novices how many times they had made their examen that day. This should not descend into morbid introspection. It is recommended really that you should have someone to help you: a director, or other trusted and experienced friend. It is possible to concentrate on one particular area or weakness and keep some sort of simple record to see what progress is being made. The idea is that by prayer and attention to the fault, its incidence will occur less often. The main point is that we are taking the problem seriously and *working* at it, because sin and weakness are nuisances. They prevent us from serving and praising God as we should and spoil our persons. They get in the way of our true natures and our true purposes and destroy our joy.

> Grant us the grace, Lord, to see what we could be and what we are. Help us to see, recognise and acknowledge our sins and imperfections, and to be genuinely sorry over them. May the Holy Spirit continue to help us and to strengthen us to lead good and holy lives. We thank You for all Your past goodness and mercy and patience. Help us to come to know You more and more.

III Commitment and growth

Ignatius left the cave at Manresa with the urgent desire to go on pilgrimage to Jerusalem. He was wearing an unobtrusive grey-brown cassock and a crucifix. He had cut his hair, nails etc. At that time one needed permission from the Pope in order to visit the Holy Land, so Ignatius embarked at Barcelona for Italy on the first stage of his journey. This was on 16 March 1523. He begged his way and eventually arrived on Palm Sunday. It was a dying Renaissance Rome that he found; a Rome that Pope Adrain was trying to reform, and one which Ignatius himself one day would help to transform. He received his letters of safe conduct, and after many adventures he eventually arrived in Jerusalem. He had a month there. 'Later', writes Hugo Rahner, 'Inigo described to his friend Favre how a consuming fire of love had thereupon seized him, as the mysteries of Christ's life and passion were renewed before his living gaze, and how as a result his resolve was strengthened to remain there for his own life'. However, he was not allowed to remain. He accepted this and returned to Italy, resolving to go back one day. He still had no clear idea of what he was to do. He wanted to preach Christ and win souls. He wanted to show to people the Christ who had been poor and humiliated. On the return journey it became clear to him that to do this effectively he would need to be better equipped and trained, so, again through many adventures which are well worth reading, he arrived back in Barcelona. A friend provided him with his keep and he went first to private tuition and then to the ordinary school where, at 33 years old, he sat down with the boys to learn and study. It was now that a desire was kindled in him to found a small brotherhood which would preach Christ and convert souls. He then went to the University of Alcala, but still carried on as he had in Barcelona helping beggars, reforming convents, giving spiritual direction etc. His activities came to the attention of the Inquisition and he was imprisoned under suspicion of heresy. He was later found to be innocent, but was told not to do any more teaching until he was properly trained. He had found that these activities had been interfering with his studies, so moved to a fresh start at the University of Salamanca. Here he was immediately involved in further controversy and once again imprisoned. He wrote: 'In the whole of Salamanca there are not so many footchains and handcuffs that I would not ask for more for God's love'. He still needed four more years study and he decided to go to Paris. He had found some companions over the years studying in Spain but none of them actually remained with him.

In Paris, his approach was much more prudent. His difficulty with French in itself restricted some of his activities (all study was in Latin). At first he was in great financial difficulties and begged in his holidays, even coming to London on one occasion. Later he found a regular benefactor, and he was able to devote more attention to his studies. He realised that study requires a certain security in material goods and in later years allowed his educational establishments to accept endowments where his parishes and missions were not allowed to accept them. Later again, he criticised some of his earlier excesses in zeal, not least because they could undermine a person's health. He was developing now a real respect for the good things of God's Creation, and using them at the same time for God's purposes. It was in Paris that he changed his name to Ignatius, after the second century martyr. He passed, and received his Master's degree from the University of Paris.

It was while he was in Paris that he eventually met six young men, one of whom was Francis Xavier. He took them one by one through the Spiritual Exercises and they were converted by them. They became his companions and the embryo of the future Society of Jesus. At the end of their studies they made vows of poverty and chastity at the little chapel of the Martyrs in the Montmartre district and resolved to go to Rome and the Holy Land. This was on 15 August 1534. Shortly after this Ignatius left the group in the charge of Peter Favre while he returned to the Basque country, ostensibly to recover his health. He was away two years — meanwhile two more people joined the group in Paris. Ignatius visited the families of the Spanish companions who had joined him, and he also set his own affairs in order. He did not stay in the family castle but in a hospice for the poor. He preached and taught children, and set in motion reforms in the local church. He set up regulations to order poor relief etc. Having made some amends for his previous bad example he took ship for Venice and there rejoined his friends who had come from Paris. They were given permission to be ordained priest and to go to Jerusalem, but no ships were available because of war with the Turks. They decided to split up into twos and go to the major cities of Italy preaching and teaching. Ignatius and two companions set out for Rome.

On their way they stopped at a small wayside shrine to Mary at La Storta. Ignatius had been praying all the time that he would be allowed to serve Christ. At this shrine he received a vision. He saw Christ, glorified, at the side of the Father, but with the cross on His shoulder. The Father said, 'I want you to take this man as your servant', and Jesus accepted him, saying, 'It is my will that you should serve us'. He also said, 'I will be favourable to you in Rome'. Ignatius received very great consolation from this vision for the rest of his life. From it arose his devotion to the name of Jesus, and he decided that his group should be called 'the Society of Jesus'. No other name was good enough. But the vision showed him Christ in glory, yes, but also carrying the cross. He knew that the way to glory always lies through the cross, through suffering. His devotion to Christ was a devotion to Christ in glory, but a glory which embraced Christ in poverty and in ignominy. For us also glory is only reached through suffering; or put it the other way round: all suffering can lead to glory. An Irish sister said to me once, 'Every little cross means a little crown'! Ignatius aimed to serve the poor and the suffering, and to share like Christ in this suffering.

The Spiritual Exercises

I have been mentioning several times in passing the Spiritual Exercises, and I want now to look more closely at these. They are 'a series of reflections, meditations and contemplations selected and arranged by Ignatius, through which the retreatant proceeds under the guidance of a director, who, in company with the retreatant, attempts to discern the Lord's present call to conversion and growth'. (Donald Reck SJ. *Review for Religious* Nov. 80 39/6). This definition shows that they were originally intended for a person making a retreat. The full way of doing them is during a 30-day retreat in a residential situation with a director. A certain amount of care and discretion should be exercised: there is a right time for doing them perhaps once or at the most twice in a lifetime. But they are adaptable and it is possible to do a shortened form over eight days; or even over three days. There is also a way of doing them during one long evening a week over an extended period.

At the beginning we considered Creation and the wonders of God revealed through it. We considered how we are part of this wonderful

Creation and how we could best play this part. All Creation is lovely and sparkling and good. And me? I was created lovable and able to love. This led on to a consideration of how I am spoiled and crippled in my efforts to love and serve and create by my sin and laziness and my selfishness. This brought us to the point of confession of sin and absolution. From this point on Our Lord Himself comes on the scene. The retreatant is led to ponder various scenes of His Life, in the way already outlined (introductory prayer etc.) and by fully imagining the scene and putting himself into it. The scenes may include the Annunciation; the Nativity; the Presentation in the Temple; Jesus' Baptism; the Temptations; healing and teaching stories; Christ walking on the water (put yourself right in the boat); the Feeding of the Five Thousand. Eventually there is the Passion and Death and finally the Resurrection.

Ignatius includes two of his own meditations. The first is the Call of the King, where he asks us to imagine Christ as a king inviting people to come and fight for him. The gist of the meditation is that we are invited to share with him the hardships of a battle campaign, the privations and the risk of injury and death, but in return we will share with him the glory when the battle is over.

The second meditation is also a military one. Ignatius describes two camps. One of them is Lucifer's. Actually, I normally adapt this one and prefer to see Lucifer a bit like J.R. of 'Dallas'. He is someone who is very powerful; knows what he wants and stops at nothing to get it. He manipulates people, buys people, treats them as things and not with any dignity and freedom and right of their own. He controls his world and directs it totally to his own ends which often involves the destruction of his opponents. The traditional meditation points out three steps which the devil plans to our downfall. First he tempts us with money. This leads to honour and status. This leads to pride. How true this is! I feel and behave totally differently if I am out with £20 in cash in my pocket than if I have come out without my purse and only have 2½p. Money *can* buy so much power in today's world. In contrast, Our Lord offers poverty, which leads to abuse, rejection and humiliations, but which has the result of humility.

The Exercises can be seen as a series of calls to the individual, to which he responds. We are first called to acknowledge God as our Creator; then we are called to repent. This is followed by the call to meditate on Christ and to get to know Him better and more intimately. The Two Standards exercise (just described) points up the difference between serving Christ and serving Lucifer and invites us to decide to serve Christ, and later on this decision takes more detailed shape in the final call to service.

Sometimes the Exercises are begun with a meditation on the call to John and Andrew, as described in John 1.35−39. John the Baptist points to Jesus and says, 'Behold, the Lamb of God'! The two men go after him; he turns and says, 'What do you want?' (What do *I* want?). They say, possibly slightly taken aback, 'Where do you live?' and go off with Him in response to His invitation, 'Come and see'. What would *I* say to him as I sat with him and talked throughout that long evening?

The aim of the Exercises is constantly to deepen our commitment to Christ. Conversion is not a 'one-off' experience. It occurs gently at all levels of our being. God's grace, God's love, has to touch all aspects of our being and our personality, and that is the work of a lifetime . If these meditations deepen or broaden our appreciation just a little they will have begun to serve their purpose.

Discernment

The way of prayer described makes a lot of use of the imagination. St. Ignatius would be the first to recognise that this is only one way of praying; in fact he suggests other ways, to be used at different times during the retreat (or at home), e.g. the 'Jesus' prayer. The advantage of the imaginative way is that our active minds and active life are brought right into the sphere of the prayer in that it is *we* who are in the scene, and this way our minds can actually be altered during the course of the meditation. This can happen in other forms of comtemplation but perhaps there the peace etc. seeps through and affects our active lives; here, there is a much more direct attack on our everyday thinking.

But when we do use the imagination, then we also open the door and admit the possibility of going 'off-key'. It is possible to get led astray, i.e. to get wrong ideas, and this is where the practice of discernment comes in. Discernment is related to discerning the call addressed to *me, now;* a call which is different from anyone else's. It may be to carry on as I am already doing, but with fresh heart and deeper understanding of it. Or it may mean a radical change of life. This is why a director is necessary. If we read the call too quickly and act on it, then we can get into all sorts of difficulties. Visions always look different when worked out in practice. The utmost care is needed to interpret correctly. One has only to think of a few ideas which have gone wrong to see the point of this. It is so easy to misread the Spirit!

Ignatius gives in the Exercises some rules for distinguishing between good and evil impulses or influences. He sees all thoughts or movements of the imagination as coming either from the good spirit or a bad spirit, and he put the rules together so that, of these influences, 'only good ones may be admitted, evil ones being rejected'. He had a very practical attitude! In these rules, he warns that the bad spirit may come as an 'angel of light', i.e. that the idea presented can seem very good — that it can objectively be a good idea — but it may not be the right idea for me, now.

I suggest there are at least three elements in Ignatius' way of discernment. The first is his consideration of consolation and desolation in prayer. The second concerns detachment; so we are not in fact wanting one course of action rather than another. The third is the use of our own right reason. Let us look in more detail at these three aspects.

The idea of discerning a right course of action through seeing whether we are consoled or depressed by the thought came to Ignatius when he was lying on his bed at Loyola recovering from his injuries. Quoting from his own autobiography (which is written in the third person): 'When he was thinking about the things of the world, he took much delight in them, but afterwards, when he was tired and put them aside, he found that he was dry and discontented. But when he thought of going to Jerusalem, barefoot and eating nothing but herbs and undergoing all the other rigours that he saw the saints had endured, not only was he consoled when he had these thoughts, but even after putting them aside, he remained content and happy . . . Little by little he came to recognise the difference between the spirits that agitated him, one from the demon, the other from God.' These thoughts are picked up in the Exercises. He says, 'For those who are making earnest progress . . . rising from good to better in the service of God Our Lord, it is typical of the evil spirit to cause regret and sadness, using fallacious arguments to disturb them and impede their progress. On the other hand, the role of the good spirit is to provide courage and strength, to console and inspire, to move to tears, all in a spirit of peace'. He goes on to describe spiritual comfort, which may move us to tears, bringing peace and joy and drawing us more towards love of God and of heavenly things, and also to describe spiritual distress, which brings restlessness, disturbance, apathy and melancholy. He adds that in times of distress or depression we should not alter anything but carry on in the state of mind and according to the decisions we made before we entered into this state. This is very wise advice and relevant to today. Later on he says: 'The characteristic effect produced by God and His angels in their spiritual operations is genuine lightness of heart and spiritual joy, eliminating all the disturbing sadness engendered by the enemy, whilst his characteristic activity is to resist such lightness of heart and spiritual comfort, alleging specious reasons, subtle suggestions and sophistries without end'. That again has a very modern and familiar ring to it! The trouble with desolation, or depression as we more often say, is that it can be so strong that we forget the consolations we have had in the past and cease to believe that we can ever be consoled in the future. That is why it is sometimes a good idea to make a note somewhere when we are consoled so that we can remember it at a later time. He advises us to pay attention to the whole of a train of thought in case the bad spirit comes in like an angel of light with a good and sound suggestion but then turns it to bad effect in us, leaving us sad and disturbed.

There is much more on the same lines. A vast amount has been said and written on this. I can do little more than just outline the areas available for exploration.

The second aspect of discernment is that of detachment which is in fact a work of a lifetime. Ignatius is after a total and deep-rooted detachment: one that constitutes a real martyrdom if taken seriously. The argument would run that if we are attached to anything — i.e. if we say, 'I will serve You *provided that* . . . You don't ask me to do this, or give up that,' etc. — then we are *not free* to the extent that we are attached to that particular condition of our service. But really to free ourselves in thought, let alone in practice, is an immensely painful operation, to be done gently, with Our Lord's help, at His pace which is in fact the only pace we can manage, i.e. it is *our* pace. The final detaching of ourselves comes, of course, at death when we leave all behind us. The natural dying process is one of stripping and detachment, and in some people we can see this process gradually and gently happening. Christian asceticism is the anticipating of this process in order to be more free to serve Christ in this life. It requires great trust on our part in the Lord. He *does* know what He is doing; He *is* kind; He *does* help us; He does restore what He takes. It only hurts us when we resist. If once He puts His finger in our lives, we can only wriggle around until we find a way to be comfortable with it. He does not move His finger.

To help us to achieve this detachment, Ignatius encourages us actually to pray *against* what we want to happen. All is subject to His will and to His greater glory, but it is still possible to try a request both ways genuinely. We have to try to be 'like a pair of scales perfectly poised, inclined neither this way nor that'. He then suggests making a list of pros and cons and, in a context of prayer and a real desire to do what is to the greater glory of God, using 'my intelligence with strict honesty', to come to a rational decision about the matter.

This leads right into the third aspect in discernment: the use of our own right reason, i.e. thinking properly about it, which includes normal moral considerations. Further suggestions he makes here include imagining a man placed in the same position as I find myself and having to make the same decision: what would I advise him? Or if I am looking back at my life from my deathbed: what would I wish to have done in this position?

Discernment all points to the making of a decision, and this making of a decision is the climax and central point of importance in the Exercises. Perhaps the reason is obvious: that such a decision actually affects our way of life, whether it means a change or whether it confirms us in an existing pattern. All our energies now can go into the way of life; none will need to be wasted in basic doubts or reconsiderations or looking over our shoulders at other people. All these things can undermine our confidence and affect our performance — and our joy.

We have reached the stage in the Exercises where the retreatant goes on to think about the Passion and Death of Our Lord. This can be done in several ways. One way is to read the whole story through from one Gospel slowly, pausing wherever you want to. Another way is to fix on one part of it: perhaps the Agony in Gethsemane; or the scene where He is brought out on

15

to the balcony by Pilate, who says, 'Behold, the man!' or even the Crucifixion itself. Is he saying anything to *me*? Do not attempt to do the whole of it — and remember: Resurrection *did* follow. The Passion now is never meant to be considered outside the context of the Resurrection.

We have already considered Ignatius at La Storta, just outside Rome, where he had the vision of Our Lord carrying the Cross but in the glory of the Trinity. He realised that for him the way to glory led through suffering. One of the first Jesuits, Jerome Nadal, wrote, 'The foundation of our Society is Jesus Christ crucified. As He has redeemed the human race by His cross, and as today He undergoes the greatest pains and crosses in His mystical body, which is the Church, so he who belongs to our Society should have no other aim than to follow Christ through persecutions without number, to procure the salvation of souls along with and in company with Christ'. The invitation of the King in the meditation mentioned earlier uses these words: 'Whoever wishes to join me in this enterprise must be willing to labour with me, so that by following me in suffering he may follow me in glory'. This affects all of us, to a greater or lesser extent, but He is with us in our suffering. There really doesn't seem any way to avoid a certain amount of suffering — but He *is* with us! He said, 'In the world you have tribulation, but be of good cheer! I have overcome the world' (Jn. 16.33).

Gracious Lord, we pray that you will help us to make any necessary decisions in our lives so that we may serve you more freely and perhaps contribute a little to your great glory.

Be with us also in our sufferings, be they big or little, and lead us through them to the joy of your resurrection life.

IV Resurrection and Service

Ignatius went on to Rome where he stayed until his death in 1556. The other companions joined him, and they gave the Exercises to people, ministered and taught. During a famine they fed and cared for thousands in the house they had been given by the Frangipani. They were again accused of heresy, but this time were cleared and completely vindicated. Soon afterwards they made a fourth vow of obedience and loyalty to the Pope. They gave up all plans for going to the Holy Land and returned the money they had been given for the purpose. In 1540 the Pope issued a Bull formally approving the name of the Society, its universal apostolate and its vow of special obedience. Ignatius was unanimously chosen as its first leader, and he eventually agreed to accept this honour. He started, amid some opposition, a home for prostitutes who wished to reform their lives, and also did a lot of writing. He died quietly without the sacraments on 31 July 1556; his companions had not realised how close to death he was. The Order had grown phenomenally. At the time of his death there were 20 houses in Italy and 19 elsewhere, and

1,000 members. Only 38 of these, in addition to the original founder members, were fully professed, which is some indication of the length of time and the care taken in their training. Ignatius was canonised in 1622, together with St. Francis Xavier.

It could be said that this final stage of his life corresponds to the final part of the Exercises, where consideration is given to the Resurrection and the beginnings of the early Church. The contemplations on the Resurrection are on the same pattern as the earlier ones. Scenes that can be taken are, for instance, His appearance to Mary Magdalene in the garden; or breakfast by the lake; or perhaps the walk to Emmaus. (How would I explain to the stranger the events which had taken place during that week of all weeks in Jerusalem? How would he explain them to me from the Scripture?) Ignatius suggests that we think about Our Lord *consoling* His friends for what they had been through.

The Exercises end with a contemplation which is at the core of his thinking: the Contemplation for Achieving Love. It is in two parts, but first he makes two preliminary observations:
1) Love is a matter of doing rather than protesting;
2) Love consists of a mutual sharing and giving — goods, honour, education etc.

He tells us first to put ourselves in the presence of God and the saints and angels who are all pleading for me. Then I should ask for what I want, which here is a deep-felt appreciation of all His goodness and blessings to me, that I may become completely devoted to Him in *effective* love.

Then I should recall all the good things I have received from Him. (It can be very helpful sometime to write our own personal 'salvation history': i.e. to record all the moments when we felt we 'grew'; or moments when He was very close; or answered us specially; or when we made some sort of decision for Him. It can include times when our faith deepened; or took a new turn. This can help us to see the pattern in our lives. We can thank Him; we can trust that it will continue.) My creation and redemption — anything that is good — has its source in Him. He has shared it with me, in love. He wants to share much more with me, if I will receive it. His love is only limited by my unwillingness and my limited capacity to receive it. He wants to share all that is in His power to share. He has shared in the past; He is sharing now; He will share because He is faithful.

It is in response to this that Ignatius raises his voice in the great prayer of self-oblation (see below, p.21).

The contemplation goes on, inviting us to:—
See God living in His creatures;
in matter, giving it existence;
in plants, giving them life;
in animals, giving them consciousness;
in men, giving them intelligence.

God is active and alive in the whole created world — and also in me! He is currently keeping me in being, and giving me existence, life, consciousness and intelligence. Even more — I am His temple, created in God's image and likeness. Ignatius then goes on and invites us to think of God actively working — energising, thrusting forth — in all creation, conferring on it existence, life, etc; continually creating them, holding them in being, all the time; *now*. This includes me: all I have and am comes ultimately from Him.

The contemplation ends with a little colloquy with the Father, or Our Lord, and perhaps a set prayer.

This 'seeing God in all things' is the mark and core of Ignatian spirituality. It is the thinking behind the action: the thinking which enables his followers to engage actively in the world — hence the very apostolic and daring enterprises of the Jesuits as against the more traditional monasticism which was mentioned at the beginning. It makes it very appropriate for lay people and for today's world. Discernment becomes relevant again because, if we are living in the world and working in it, we need to be able to see our way through it. We want to be able to recognise right directions and true and authentic growth and development amid a wealth of false and mock growth. A lot of damage is done through conversation. Every time we say something we don't really mean we take ourselves a step further away from who we really are and strengthen the false self within us. Silence is better! (even though it can offend). Shallow talk is no talk; our real self sinks deeper within us. With how many people do we really communicate? We don't always want to. There doesn't always seem to be time. It may be that we are most at risk in this area. We treat people as things and indulge in jargon and communiqué rather than take time for proper communication. The world needs truth: truth in speech, truth in relationships, truth and recognition of truth in action. Only in this way will the false be undermined.

Praying in solitude deepens our awareness of truth, and heightens our sensitivities, so that when we re-engage with the world we are more able to pray and live in a Christian way right *in* it and contribute to its authentic, proper and God-intended growth. We will be less likely to be led astray by illusion: 'deceits of the devil' (1 Timothy 4:1); false goals. How are we going to combat gross materialism unless we have first done so in our own hearts and lives? Pray God that He will help us.

In Ignatius' last years in Rome he wrote the Constitutions of the Society of Jesus and he wrote into them these principles of being deeply committed to Christ, and of being contemplative in the world, i.e. in active mission and service and creativity. That is why the Society was so revolutionary in its day. It was very much adapted to the needs and conditions of the emerging, complex and growing new world, the beginning of our modern world. See also how his early zest for life had been taken up in his vision of living the Christian life. Jesuits are encouraged to use the good things of creation if they help the work forward and contribute to God's greater glory.

The Society from the first has contained great missionary activity. Jesuits (who include the great St. Francis Xavier) penetrated India, China, Japan, North America, Canada etc. The British Province has included Zimbabwe and Guyana. Nearer at home, they became chaplains to Courts (hence the many accusations of political intrigue), ran schools, taught in Universities, set up parish missions. There was always meant to be some missionary aspect to their work; thus they are found today in city centres rather than in ordinary parishes. They did not say the office in choir like all other orders of their day: they were not allowed stable incomes in any works apart from educational work. Hence they could go anywhere at any time (in principle) and *be available* to the ordinary people they wished to serve. They also provided notable theologians to the Council of Trent (the Council of the Counter-Reformation, that reaffirmed doctrine, tightened up discipline and restricted abuses in the RC Church). They helped keep the Roman Catholic Faith alive in England and many were martyred.

Ignatius' principles, i.e. the Constitutions, were later adopted by any number of active orders. Today, the Jesuits are still trying to adapt to the new challenges of the modern world. They were prominent among the theologians at Vatican II in 1962, the Council which is doing so much in opening out the Roman Catholic Church today.

But what about us? We are not Jesuits and are never likely to be. Has Ignatius any message for us? Obviously, yes. We have seen that the Church appears to have two possibilities, complementary, not contradictory. It can provide a haven, sanctuary or escape from the world; or it can become the leaven in the lump working with the world and in the world for God's kingdom of peace and justice in actual fact. It doesn't matter that it may not happen in actual terms in any definitive way in this world. As a person works for his individual growth and health yet in the end dies, so we work for true growth, culture, health and peace in global terms, even though we know that it will not be consummated, i.e. will not find final expression, until the next world, after the end or the destruction of this.

Whilst not denying the necessity and reality of the Church as a refuge, as I read the signs, we are being asked as a Church also to involve ourselves in the life and death struggles of the actual world. For each individual this participation in the struggle will take place in a different arena, but if we find we are struggling in *no* arena, then I think it is the time seriously to re-assess our Christian position, to check that we are not mere bystanders watching a drama in which we think we participate actively, but in which we in fact participate negatively by our very inactivity.

What are these challenges that the world presents to us today? What are the insistent voices from both secular and ecclesiastical circles to which we are bound to listen? I think that from all sides the problems of peace and of unity are the most pressing, both of which link integrally with questions of justice. The immense moral problems arising from a world where two thirds are in real deprivation and one third is in considerable wealth and luxury, and spending vast amounts of money on weapons which, at the decision of a minute number of people, can effectively destroy the world for everyone, *must* draw some response from us. Thank God that it is doing so. These concerns for peace and justice are shown by Christians and non-Christians alike. There is a growing awareness in all churches of the need to speak out on these issues and to act in issues concerning life and liberty; issues concerning oppression, torture, exploitation etc. Nevertheless, the issues are rarely clear-cut, and the Church will only be able to speak prophetically and wisely as it deepens its own allegiance and conscious commitment to and dependence on Christ Our Lord — Christ poor, humiliated and rejected, yet glorious and powerful in His Resurrection. Hence the need for constant recourse to prayer, the Bible and the sacraments, to strengthen and feed us in our active apostolate.

The other great challenge to the Church and the world of today is the challenge to unity. The world itself is becoming more and more aware of its own essential unity, despite conflict and disharmony everywhere. This unity is brought about by the ease of travel: by television and other communications systems; by trade and economics. Radical disagreement and disharmony among Christians becomes more and more obvious in this context and increasingly a scandal.

Quoting from Ephesians 3: 'His purpose he set forth in Christ, as a plan for the fullness of time: to unite all things in Him, things in heaven and things on earth'. Perhaps we are nearing the fullness of time, hence the move to unity in matters religious and secular. How dare we resist it?

I merely point these two areas out as challenges which seem very directly to be presented to us at the moment: the challenge to justice and peace; the challenge to unity. Surely we have a responsibility to work in both these areas.

A third challenge which occurs to me is the challenge of the great numbers of lonely people today, and the great numbers of people with no religious faith. This is one to which we can all respond directly. We can look for opportunities to communicate; to help; to care.

It is easy to be discouraged and overwhelmed by the immensity of these problems. Let us return to Our Lord, who faced the greatest challenge of all time: the cosmic overthrow of evil. He *won* the battle. The skirmishes continue, and will do so until the end of time, but we are on the winning side. He asks of us no more than we can do: in fact, He says that if we engage in immense activity and He loses our love in the process, He will count it a bad bargain. Ultimately the challenge is a challenge to individuals to unite with Him and let Him work rationally and intelligently through us, in love.

Let us renew with thanks our dedication to Him in St. Ignatius' words: —

Take and receive, Lord, all my liberty, my memory, my understanding, my entire will. You have bestowed on me whatever I have or possess. I return all back to You, and deliver it to You to be entirely subject to Your will. Only grant me Your love and Your grace, and I am rich enough, and ask for nothing more.

Acknowledgments

St. Ignatius of Loyola   Leonard von Matt & Hugo Rahner S.J.
                                       trans. John Murray S.J.
                                       (Henry Regnery Co. Chicago 1956)

The Autobiography of St. Ignatius Loyola
                                       Trans. Joseph F. O'Callaghan
                                       Ed. John C. Olin
                                       (Harper Torchbooks 1974)

Review for Religious   November 1980. 39/6

The Spiritual Exercises of St. Ignatius Loyola
                                       Trans. Thomas Corbishley S.J.
                                       (Anthony Clarke 1973)

Suggestions for further reading

DIVARKAR, P.   The Path of Interior Knowledge
Gujarat Sahitya Prakash, 1982

FLEMING, D.   Modern Spiritual Exercises
Doubleday Image, & Institute of Jesuit
Sources, 1978

GREEN, T.H.   Weeds Among the Wheat
Ave Maria Press, 1984

HAUSER, R.J.   Moving in the Spirit
Paulist Press, 1986

HEWETT, W.   Inigo: Story & Songs (cassettes)
Inigo Centre, 1981

HUGHES, G.W.   God of Surprises
Darton Longman & Todd, 1985

VELTRI, J.   Orientations Vol. I
Loyola House, Guelph, 1979

YOUNG, W.   St. Ignatius's Own Story
Loyola University Press, 1980

Information about making the *Spiritual Exercises* for longer or shorter periods may be obtained from The National Retreat Centre, Liddon House, 24 South Audley Street, LONDON W1Y 5DL (01 – 493 3534).